IN THE ZERO OF SKY

TAMRA PLOTNICK

ASSURE PRESS

Copyright © 2021 by Assure Press

All Rights Reserved. No part of this book may be performed, recorded, used or reproduced in any manner whatsoever without the written consent of the author and the permission of the publisher except in the case of brief quotations embodied in critical articles and review.

ASSURE PRESS

An imprint of

Assure Press Publishing & Consulting, LLC

www.assurepress.org

Publisher's Note: Assure Press books may be purchased for educational, business, or sales promotional use. For information please visit the website.

In the Zero of Sky/ Tamra Plotnick— 1st ed.

Cover Art by Camille Laoang

ISBN-13: 978-1-7356923-8-8
Library of Congress Control Number: 2020943798
eISBN-13: 978-1-7356923-9-5

THANK YOU

Family, you have been a pulsing nest of love:
Yariv, Ty, Tazha, Lois, Paul, Mark, Carina, Skai, Eliaz, Zeb, Elaine, Luke, Amadeus, Lorelai, Ruth, Sam, Mildred, Sam, Francine, Joyce, Carey, Hal, Sandy, Carol, Tanz, Steve, Rosalie, Selma, Pearl, Rosanna, Mamisa, Sapphire, Suzanne

Thank you

Friends and Colleagues in Teaching, Art and Life, for your support and your witness:
Isabel, Mindy, Camille, Poonam, Stephanie, Anath, Peggy, Alexandra, Ilka, Pam, Joe, Annie, Judy, Kris, Lisa, Claudia, Idoia, Jehu, Estella, Netta, Brett, Gabe, Maria-Jesus, Patricia, Regina, Elga, Cassia, Dan, Marie, Marie France, Roberto, Shelly, Jules, Rehana, David, Seth, Abby, Athena, Stacey, Ashley, Sherry, Kelly, Tyler, Linda, TJ, Sharon, Natalie, Hannah, Shana, McKenzie, Christine, Brady, Steven, Caity, Katie, Jerry, Luiggi, Sean, Angela, Nakeeba, Tabari, Ellie, Jennifer, Tanine and so many other dears from JBS, STAR, BCHS, Pace and BEGIN

Thank you

Students, you have taught me volumes:
Zahira, Mikayla, DI, Rokeya, Tamara, Tania, Heaven, Nickesia, Oludare, you stand for over a thousand individuals who, as my students, have been my teachers

Thank you

Mentors, in person or from the page or the ages, for sharing your light:
Grace Paley, Linsey Abrams, Barry Wallenstein, EM Broner, Claudia Dreyfus, Veena Oldenburg, Cheryl Clarke, Cheryl Boyce Taylor, Pedro Pietri, Bob Holman, Delphine Delbello Spencer,

Pat Hall, Rosangela Silvestre, Frank Ricci, Maria Mar, Ms. Alford, Joy Silver, Jennifer Wolfe, Tracy K. Smith, Edwidge Danticat, Toni Morrison, James Baldwin, Joy Harjo, Sandra Cisneros, Octavio Paz, Cesar Vallejo, Pablo Neruda, Octavia Butler, Emma Goldman, Hannah Senesh, Harriet Tubman

Thank you

Darius Frasure and Assure Press, for selecting and delivering this work, and to all of those who have volleyed smiles, wisdom, goodwill and love with me in this lifetime

Thank you

ACKNOWLEDGMENTS

"Afternoon without Children" *Stickman Review* V15 N1
"At Night" *Caprice*, July 1995
"Blustery" *LiveMag* Issue 13 Fall 2016
"Chariot" *Lowestoft Chronicle* Sept. 2017 Issue 31
"The Buddha Might Be in Brooklyn" *The Midwest Quarterly* Spring 2018
"Da New York Sky" *BigCityLit* Fall 2017
"Diamond Snow" *Right Hand Pointing*, April- Part II 2018
"Golpes after Vallejo" *The Raw Art Review* Winter 2020
"The Eternal Saga of Fear vs. Freedom" *Lurch* Winter 2014
"Jazz Jungle" *Tribes* #8, 1998
"Maternal Nature" *Poetry in Performance* 25, 1997
"No" *Poetry in Performance* 33, 2005
"Night Blossom" *BigCityLit* Fall 2017
"Silhouette" *The Madison Review* Fall 2016 Vol. 39 no. 1
"signs of god and art in Barcelona" *Atlanta Review* Vol. XXIII No. 2
"Spanish House" *Saint Mark's Poetry Project Newsletter*, Feb/Mar 1988
"Thanks for the Bouquet Billy" *Poetry in Performance* 31, 2003
"The Ultimate Meet Up" *Stickman Review* Spring 2016
"When the Moon Loses 500 Degrees" *Serving House Journal* Fall 2016

For Yariv, Ty and Tazha

CONTENTS

IN THE ZERO OF SKY

Blustery	3
Beautiful Music	4
Day Winks Randomly	5
By the Sea Bed	6
Reprise	7
Blackbird, the Sky	8
LA LA Land	9
Painter at Seventy	11
Da New York Sky	12

OUR OWN OBLIVIOUS SHADOW

when the moon loses five hundred degrees	17
Thanks for the Bouquet Billy	18
Jazz Jungle	19
Observations Upon Returning to New York	20
Silhouette	21
The Buddha Might Be in Brooklyn	22
A Midwinter Midnight, Downtown	23
Williamsburg Walking the Line	24
Spring Glances at Park	25

A WOMAN'S GARDEN OF VERSUS

A Woman's Garden of Verses	29
Autobiography of an Ordinary Artist	31
The Liberation of Words	32
Afternoon without Children	34
Maternal Nature	35
we wake up	36
No	37
The Ultimate Meet Up	38
Night Blossom	40

ORIGINS

origins	43
Ode to the House Cat	44
after Dickinson	45
Fire Angel: The Bellydancer	46
in case of severe amnesia read this	47
Spanish House	48
Spanish Lunch	49
essay	50
The Gospel According to Snowflakes	51

ETERNAL SAGA

diamond snow	55
The Eternal Saga of Fear vs. Freedom: Verse 1: Lake Monster Mongering	56
Chariot	57
Cupid Imposter Mistakes Heart for Rotten Apple	58
Golpes after Vallejo	59
Mugged but not Held	61
terrible, this love	62
Personal Prisms	64
Tragically	65
dullness and evil	66
Past.perfect	67

VOW

Vow	71
Signs of God and Art in Barcelona	72
Morning Prayer	73
The Whispering Woods	74
Palmistry	75
The Cradle of My Mother's Hips	76
All Hands	77
Comfort Zone	78
Without Preaching	79
At Night	80

About the Author

IN THE ZERO OF SKY

Blustery

how I flutter from far
in the zero of sky
without wings without words
without engines, birds
vague that I know
Brooklyn Bridge I go by
without eyes without ears
without heart, fear
how I enter the thingless
the flying, the thing
without speed without speech
no blood nor crutch
from the concrete and glass
and my surrogate self
in my job in my clothes
in my day in my doze
my selfless I send
while I don't comprehend
how that flash in the blue
be it paper or ghost
as it soars, sucks me up
till I'm hugged by the high
by the wind
and I'm nothing
(that thing)
in the zero of sky

Beautiful Music

moon as gull wing
   caught on   breath of
       wind

leave us still   here
     move, the earth, so   soar
slide   the groove of
     universe

like on you I

like I never thought
   but US
      elongated, curled

and then   YOU
    let the butterfly
      loose in me

I catch, draw
   like not before

Day Winks Randomly

—at you.
A butterfly.
What a flirt.

By the Sea Bed

Ocean's
vast turquoise
blanket bats her
frill lash at me
Electric sea horse
banters by a Bahamian
*Can't hear with these
shades on* I claim
his arm lassos me
casual as the sun
glasses off, I say
*Five more minutes
on the land*
Peace says he
Sky unfurls his
smoky lining
kicking
up sand I
tuck myself in
the enormous wet
blue
canopy
bed

Reprise

In the airplane I play
you back at will

see your tree trunk
bold, branching
into my sky.
flushed, I draw
last night's breath
into this day

Blackbird, the Sky

Blackbird, roving hole
in the jaundiced sky
see her
see through

Blackbird, prick night
of day blue life
lash of your blink, her flight
far-fringed wing,
wind, tethered night
Blackbird shot
through the cloud sunk sky
distant frenzy to your quiet mind
and she dives
she dives

LA LA Land

Supershuttled to N. Genesee Ave lawn
there sprawled like a spider caught
in velcro facing a fetid whiff
passerby says
Mandy, I'm so disappointed in you.
That is *so* not you
To his dog

Bougainvillea crawl over abandoned lot
another ribbon candy of discarded 16mm film
festoons dirt, weed, Coke cans

in cleavage of Hollywood Hills
high hidden canyons, where walkers send dogs
cartwheeling down precipices after tennis balls
they're startled when threatened with the SPCA

homeless, drooling guy: has a suntan, a wheelchair, a dog
lives on the beach and sings
thus appears wealthier than new-york-down-and-outers

wide, suburban-span city
stretched between petite pastel houses
strips of asphalt hold all apart like spokes

tales of lowriders, ghettomobiles as art
decked in rotating doors and rockets
for horns, Chicano power

cocktails in a Hollywood cottage
the boys say: Tom Cruise is as gay as the day is long
over tender knuckles of shrimp and gin

What's not to like

upon emerging under the azure sky
pierced with piney palms
yet the dearth of pedestrians
hints a human-wasting bomb

Painter at Seventy

Matty
hands like
heavy birds
ostriches
meaty flourishes
run fast
but don't fly

Da New York Sky

Chrysler Building
mercury injects sky
I'm sayin
why he leave me dry,
Foolish and still more foolish
lendin me ears
to da growls of da street
and me lips to da gossip
nevermind da love

I hear da chatter
Girl says:
Vinnie dyin to see
that goddam skirt on me
Boy says:
gimme milk on consignment
Da old man shouts:
I got AIDS and I bite

And I got nuttin but ta
lap it up
and save it
and say it

Cuz if I listen
to da old silver sky
I hear its blue linin'
Howlin' from behind
And its twin, sea
bellows back at me
tells me where it got him
tucked in da arms of waves

And I'm left

like a crazy one
wavin'
at da New York sky

OUR OWN OBLIVIOUS SHADOW

WHEN THE MOON loses five hundred degrees

is it milk drinking ink
or ink
drinking the moon

for whom else
shines the moon a few
loose souls
fallen like change
out the pockets
of the earth
clocking
our own oblivious
shadow
sour-faced
newyorker every newcomer
pucker-eyed
did you see
the eclipse?

Thanks for the Bouquet Billy

There's a man in Manhattan
that might be mentally naked
before you

His storefront cavern, red
by thread of Asia's Himalayas and
purple mirth of masks basked gold
in the glare of collective amnesia

Blind to the blues you might choose

There with the red behind his head
peacock there in
this giant man-made vagina, carpeted
in blood of your Blackest
most Southern music

He'll take you in
and talk jazz
till you smell your soul

Jazz Jungle

the song is a tree house
I'm in there with the drummer, a son of the island
he's frantic, snatching at cymbals
like far limbed fruit,
guanabana and papaya glistening

giant ants skedaddle down base line vines
monkeys Charleston over keyboards

I'm some girl climbing uninvited with girl germs and
her skirt caught in a branch, panties mooning
The drummer is the boy gathering and tossing
sticks He built this tree house
He knows which twig will send
it crashing

then fast the brass
plants a twister in the midst
whips up a frenzy of skirt, sticks
friction, instant fascination with girl germs
in the gnash of a tree house smashed
mirth in the
mash of boyish destruction

wind blows an exit
son shakes a downed branch
til the last leaf
falls
to hush
like the lost lover of a listener

Observations Upon Returning to New York

dead things fly
like the feet of Preserved Fish
one who's name's *porque*
we may never know
but who passed I'm sure
as we did First Avenue
to see white patent shoes,
pigeon-toed, dangled off
some invisible hugeness,
crossing

nothing like a blatant ghost
to recall life,
the slapstick potency of it,
the chatter of park birds
through windows and
windowgate hearts

his hair'd grown out
like the floss of bone men
long under.
And the pigeon perched
like raven in the hearts
of the urban
had flown off.

Silhouette

Don't shirk your own shadow
like you'd lick a lollipop
to pure pop no lolly-
gagging
pure purpose
you
are shiny
with
sheer
white
light

You might gag on
Your shadow: hung on a rack
Like a tortured lie
left
lackluster

Your shadow: a shadow of
its former self
now that God had his way with you

I do miss that murky mister
the underside of fists that flicker
like flames before they charred
to the tar black
underbelly
of your whisper

The Buddha *Might* Be in Brooklyn

for the students of BCHS past, present and future

I tell my students: "Words on a page give you points."
What I mean is that
slapping the thoughts onto the mat, that wrestling mat called a
page, actually
    creates the thoughts
What I mean is that sometimes in quantum physics, a particle is
    only there if you see it
Like if a tree falls in Brooklyn
    or even grows there
It's only *there* if someone sees it
And a word is only a thought or an artifact of soul
If a page was there to catch it
    a brain was there to spawn it
    a question was asked
    a pause was breached in the static wall that is our lives
bricked up with smart texts
strobing zones packed with Internet bars intermittent cable
infomercial coupons chasing icons
down a virtual tunnel of unstoppable sewage smoky and stoned
flushing our soft floating spirits
like noodles into the mouth of a giant plastic Buddha, which is
actually a huge Trojan toilet, not
truly Zen
      only a crashing forest of trees where Brooklyn once stood
but no one was there to hear
them fall because no one captured on a page the deforestation of
Bushwick which razed the
thoughts of generations who needed paper to crumple
when the future students of Brooklyn
were asked to put words on a page to make points

A Midwinter Midnight, Downtown

Crystal plugs in the universe,
stars don't gaze back
don't fix numbers
chart no path

o'er the Church in the Bouwerie
Saturn swiveling in his telescope,
a dollar a peep, the rings slip off an eyeball
with chill's gratuitous tear
   Painted on?
   What d'ya take me for?
   Street astronomer?

Chapped fists punch
empty pockets
while laughing.
the glass moon, high and cold

Williamsburg Walking the Line

No I will not say hello to your fantasy
as factories manufacture weather
batting over the East River
though these tattoo mold-the-butt
pants as the sun drops its own
on the barrio reveals
obscene blares of red
the workers go home
dealers arise
hookers begin to gleam
and the sirens again to whine

Spring Glances at Park

The park sinks, green wrinkled palm,
'twixt silver buildings like
extra long nails tickling the sky.
while on fortune's lines,
white collars coffee recess
over cement paths,
impotently ushering wind, (drunk on
aroma of *madrugada* off an unshowered neck,
mocking the jonquils--
so sweet they gotta be sarcastic)

April's dainty wooden fingers pinch cocktail blossoms.
barer branches kick cool air, legs of a woman long upside down
dived under packed earth.
the hollow--gape--empty of offspring.
an early bee helicopters by. No birds
bungle crumbs near momentary guru,
(tosser swathed in plaids, prints and poncho),
lost flock to toddler haunt.
Pigeons taunt flightless birds
decaled on storefront glass--
For once (Ha!) better than seagulls

Three American flags vigorous in wind
like dead veterans whistling.
Platoon of tulips salutes.
Lined up wire trash cans, the tanks.
Red tie, metronome to manager.
Cars on horn.
Trash spearers do percussion--
(each chip bag crunch).
Heels, the castanets
rule fuschia sway of hips
'neath dew-glossed lips.

She takes her game with her,
while fellas on benches
roll eyes sideways
like precious marbles.

A WOMAN'S GARDEN OF VERSUS

A Woman's Garden of Versus

as women
tend
my soul I
leased
relinquished
persona
truths
mind idled
interminably
or till
indeterminable
age
of growth
or youth grown
husband's well
groundswell
planted
household
sprouted
labors
tabled
fabled hands
folded
binge of blather
stabled
or until
escape
valved
skills
shifted
tangents
reverted
targets
aborted

weeds of wisdom
thwarted
my soul I
tend

Autobiography of an Ordinary Artist

I would sweep the walk
to frock the air
in dust blouses

each plate stacked at
ninety percent symmetry,
the bowls invert

how many hounds
could a hammer howl down
to pound down a nail

once I browned onions
to lace edges
the garlic I kept raw

in those days
I was interested in any word
beginning with Z

The Liberation of Words

Can words,
the slaves of the working woman,
Rebel from their ordering
tasks and rename the universe
with unseen possibility?

Can I release
monstrosities
safely sequestered
in prisons of flesh
and thought?

Will secrets
unbeknownst
in the soldiering
of the quotidian
crawl from beneath
this pristine sheet?

Do dreams incarnate
once dripped
bit by bit
onto the creamy canvas
of the leaf?

Or can the faith
of the abstinent
ignite and,
like tongues of flame,
surge to disregard
those metal bars of logic
that restrained it
for so long
only to cavort

in the open
like fiery gossips?

Afternoon without Children

I ask for wisdom
But crave rage
What if I crumple these wishes
In my serving palms
And toss them
Away

I can be no one
Without children
Running through my
Empty corridors

My breath
Has no true desire
But a path
Wearied and worn
Instinct for life

I drop all quests
Just now
The endless searching
Yawns in my bones
I pray for rest

But fear the long grey
Nothingness
Of it

Maternal Nature

beneath the ripest fruit, your ears
your regal sweep nose, a hawk
down the whisker-framed purple pout come scowl
under eyelids, fringed with black luxurious lash,
   that drolly shade
   anybody home
away within the muscular canoe of you,
   The hirsute torso I've ridden
   far on furious rivers
Rests a perfect papoose
your blinking baby boy
My Love my urge
   To take you back
   To take you way back
   And cradle you
   like the moon
   that's only out for you
   And rock you to
   a more auspicious astrology

WE WAKE up

—women
our souls
crumpled
in someone's fist

we are journeying cold
concealing

a blizzard of loneliness
hands that cradle
everything
but our own
souls
crumpled
in someone's fist

we are carpenters without tools
beggars with trickle down fingers

we are
a satin skinned embrace, raw hands
in warring weather
a temple

come in
be holy

No

There's nothing like a strong woman.
A strong knock-out woman.
Who can knock-out men.
Strong and tall enough to look like a man.
Or a boy. A pretty boy.
She might be knocked out if bigots take her for a boy.

And then there's nothing like her pain
to stir tenderness in the soul you were keeping
for your rainy day wedding.
There's nothing like a woman who looks
like a boy to make you want to marry a woman.
Even if you are one.

No. Nothing like her arms around you strong.
She can pick you up. Hold you like your own skin.
There's nothing like trying to collect up her long
muscular limbs and fold her like a babe into your embrace.

There's no one like a strong woman when she cries.
Nothing like wet crystals over stone cheekbones.
You want to ride them down her face.
You want to land in her heart. But you'll settle for her pocket.
Cause she's strong and she's sad and she's weak in front of you.
And you're already in her pocket but she doesn't know it.

No. There's nothing like turning yourself inside out
and emptying yourself into her pocket.
There's no one like her, who wouldn't at least check the pocket
for a tissue. But you've already given her one.
And you should have emptied yourself into her heart anyway.

The Ultimate Meet Up

So I walk into this dive
And there I am.
Don't get me wrong
I'm not the ultimate narcissist, but
I am very attracted.
So I offer to buy
Myself a drink.

I'm a teetotaler,
Answers Myself.

Dang, you're good.
Too good.
Almost pure,
I retort.

I know what you mean,
Replies the other Me,
But I'm not sure it's
getting me anywhere.

Anywhere?
Where do you want to go?

That's just it.
I don't really know.
Probably nowhere.
I massage my eyelids
the way I do
when I'm thinking hard enough
to forget about smudging eyeliner.
I take a generous breath.
Yea, says Me, Nowhere might be
the ultimate destination.

Oh I see, I say.
There's a long pause
and then I tell Myself,
I think you have arrived.

Night Blossom

"You're the mean and gentle flower
in my sentimental night"[1]
Though your countenance is dour
your aroma conjures blithe
petals shooting scarlet toward an unsuspecting sky
Like a field, I lie beneath you wond'ring when your bud will ply.
As I languish in the shadow
of your stingy dearth of words,
my vestal garden's fallow,
my forlorn caress perturbs
the apathetic timbre of your inward gazing eyes
till your stamen grows to wander and your stamina surprise.

---

1. Barry Wallenstein

ORIGINS

ORIGINS

how music happens:

strong girls
pluck their limbs
against the stripes
of the sea

how light happens:

a thousand cold goblets
knock back
against the sea's spine
and beg for gold

how there is sand:

each ancient wave
comes to the edge
spits a tooth

ODE to the House Cat

villanelle for Pali

Your provenance hints of a regal past
Four pawed and yet you sail as if with wing
The lack of your compunction looms so vast

While boxing even dogs remain outclassed
When you slink out of nowhere children cringe
Your provenance hints of a regal past

As servant you have trained me to be fast
I've learned to keep my needs and wants as fringe
The lack of your compunction looms so vast

You're Eye of Ra: the goddess dye is cast
Any attempt to stare down will unhinge
Your provenance hints of a regal past

When flesh you score you leave my heart aghast
Yet useless to pursue you and avenge
The lack of your compunction looms so vast

Like 'gyptian cats all evil you outcast
Yet wicked sprites you reek of just a tinge
Your provenance hints of a regal past
The lack of your compunction looms so vast

after Dickinson

Love is the thing with fangs
That nips you in your sleep
And ravaged, seeks to drain
Your every resource deep

It overtakes so regally
The loveseat in your chest
And languor's there—'gainst your decree
Its fur requires a pet

And were you to adore its puss
So snuggle to its soul
It toasts your nights with none but looks
Then tears your flesh with claw

Fire Angel: The Bellydancer

for Anath

The spark:
glint off the eye
twist of lash
permanent wink
the expression
a lotus
vacillating
atop invisible sun-glazed pond

The flicker: feather fingers that possess ethereal magma
as if she yoyos a plum comet
from one wing
to the other

The flame:
molten midriff
stretched like hot taffy across
the soul, insinuating
an amorous
dialectic
between
heart and hip

IN CASE of severe amnesia read this

remember the air is pushing hard as it can against the walls
though it is as frail as the breath of humming bird
the sky drops it down hard as it can upon our heads
that's a lot of humming birds breathing down our necks

remember there's been a continual drum beat since the
first hand
slapped dirt

Spanish House

arc of stucco
techo de tejas
and strange, the dog
called Martyr
pacing on it

a baby's giggle
rolls out from the plaza
enters the kitchen
a trill, the flap of shutters

and strange
the steam of ghosts,
dead horses and pigs
that once trod
the ground floor

Spanish Lunch

As *sesos*
are brains
and while eating hers
María-Jesús
bit on some gristle
What's this, she cried
A thought, I replied

ESSAY

    Rhythm and timbre
              of your countryside
                          INFORM
                          The music
cicadasong
clickclicking
your nervous mother's nails
w h o o s h   of   c i g a r e t t e
                  Shuffle and jabber J train
                  On overhead tracks

       $b_r i_s t_l i_n g$ $b_a b_y$ $b_u f_f a_l o$ $h_i d_e s$

    flap in your mind

  tweet of kitten
under walls and blanket of country
     house

             or are the stars
             humming tonight

The Gospel According to Snowflakes

We are a society
Of icy splinters
A society no less
A primping palace in pirouette,
A molecule of a mandala
A medallion of luck
Shrieking to ourselves in glee

We spike the air with our chorus
of pinpoint
Screeching
Scratchiti the world with
Pure crystalline love

Some call us flakes

ETERNAL SAGA

DIAMOND SNOW

horses escaping a forest fire during the Russian revolution
frozen in angst as the lake blinked to ice on impact

The Eternal Saga of Fear vs. Freedom: Verse 1: Lake Monster Mongering

Lurking in oily infinity
   (only it's water
      and a hemmed in lake)
And out of the olive black
   Skin of water
   (only it's inside, beneath and underneath)
Exists a tremendous
   And querulous presence
   (only it's transparent and nonexistent)
Yet it grips me...almost
   Just beneath my flippering feet
   Echoing *port de bras*
Embrace of freedom
   In the form of fresh
   Aqueous lapping
Lurks (I did say, you'll recall) the invisible
   Unnamable
   Unfathomable
   Darker, greener, wetter,
   Deeper evil
Ineffable chaser
   of infinity

Chariot

Love is a chariot
of the mind
galloping to distant territories
where you don't know
the language
nor the customs

But Love blazes
her own trail
and her sheer swashbuckling
can get you trading valuables,
swapping provisions,
bartering for shelter
and fleshly favors

The language of relationships,
    treaties, diplomacy
will be called for later… maybe
and may require translators,
guidebooks or ethnographies

Cupid Imposter Mistakes Heart for Rotten Apple

Someone uprooted my aorta
like a casual carrot pulled up
by a country boy, a snack
but bitter tossed and a romp
in the wilds with tropical music
winds off the coast of Cuba

Someone sprung a leak in
my internal fountain
sharp, the twang shot me
off funk guitar, of course
I saw the cherub's bow, damn
but he was thin with eyes like
the devil's medallions

Golpes after Vallejo

*"Hay golpes en la vida tan fuertes..."**
not tiny insults like the cat's claw
piercing your sweet big toe
till it spouts crimson tears
You are sturdy and have antiseptic
The cut is but an inch in your miles and miles of life

Still
"Hay golpes en la vida tan fuertes..."
Blows so hard in life
So strong

"Hay golpes ..."
they shot off his face
that boy, so pure and golden
fresh from the island when I first knew him
now a man, a father
who cannot stand whole for his progeny:
three children
two stateside, one on the island

Yes
"Hay golpes en la vida tan fuertes..."
Blows so hard in life
So strong

"golpes ..."
they severed his identity
one bullet that sliced through his face
amputating the chin, half the mouth
half his face fell off,
the jaw bones, left splintered
died

Hay golpes en la vida tan fuertes...

Blows so hard
Perhaps not softened but cushioned
By a sister who unravels miles and miles of life
To cocoon this shattered man
To wrap those *golpes en la vida*
in the endless silk
of her love

* Line from Cesar Vallejo

Mugged but not Held

> two bodies face to face
> are at times two stones
> and night a desert
>
> - OCTAVIO PAZ

Mugged
knife point
pricked night
rocket ready
to take us

the bridge is always a desert

our bed is a bridge
we're crossing in opposite directions

I'm gone over
this next day, still moneyed
in the city,
snaky with arms,
short of
your embrace.

TERRIBLE, this love

        missing bleeds through
        dampens
        twenty seconds past
        his kiss
        inhaled diagonal musk
        down wiry chest

        urgently
        this poem broadcasts
        pretending
        future ears
        will be lured without
        fear of love's flesh
        no face of consternation
        between them

        perfectly
        his almond eyes
        hang beneath
        black arching lash
        betray
        cruel innocence while
        purple half moon lips
        on the rise
confirm, as ingenuous as nature
        as potent
        his jagged tooth no stranger
        to gravity, the dumb
        and hopeless prism
        of pain

        how readily I
        duck under
        elegance, his fringed brow

conspire
to get intimate
with shadows, delay
the garish play
of sun's glare

Personal Prisms

Impetuous and Meticulous
   went for a ride, discussing
Tenacious meets Spontaneous for lunch
   and gossip:
Whimsical goes out with Curmudgeon
   every now and then
   dying, however, for
Ingénue, who sees herself as Crone of a sudden
   while
Bulimic wrestles with Blasé
   basically every day
   unaware that
Self-righteous shares the bed with Gullible
   who takes it in stride that
Sister Simpleton makes coffee for Conspiracy Theorist
   disabused of the fiction that
Angelic surfs the same waves as Risqué
   who doubles as
Arrogant catching a bus full of Duteous
   who wish to be Studious rowing boats with Flippant
   not deigning to wonder at
Lascivious who studies under Monk

Tragically

Tragically
your unctuous is
my magnanimous

Your phony is
my heartfelt
your corny, my soulful

your TMI, my intimate
your flaky, my whimsical
your tacky
my funky
your selfish
my centered

and yet we reside on the same stage
in the same friendship
same marriage,
bed
body

DULLNESS AND EVIL

Saturday rain wriggles from the sky
shushing superfluous sound effects
interfering with alpha waves
and other grey matters
worms and germs
ants have no homes
slick traffic ferries away your most corrugated thoughts
the crack the crack the broken Momma's
black nylon winged
UMBRELLA
untouched
in a quiet corner
erupts *evil*
as the smirk on a cape
colorless and canned
like the belief you can think
yourself out of
a mean
afternoon

Past.perfect

Someone. was knocking on her face. That morning
she ran. Over a dead pair of trousers.

Past tense. all night ink
she could smell. God in that room
he. Was a boy clone of her.
A lost twin on the low road

after she left him. having never been with him
years later. she had her heart. broke by him
there. that's translated.
Fill in the blanks with. E.S.P. or put. IT THIS WAY:
the one she trusted to always lie betrayed her
the one she robbed of a chance to betray her
gave it away like loose change to Jews for Jesus

Present.tense. all day. harrowing,
separate. solar. systems. imagine. who's? the star!
There're still twins though

he lives in a dead pair of trousers
his real house. the high rise projects
an imposter. he wears no shoes whenever possible. There.
after all these half years. She. still. writes him love poems.

Past. perfect. pulled. an all. nighter.
HAD THEY KNOWN. THEY'D. HAVE NEVER
GUESSED GREASY DINERS AND LIFE STORIES LIKE
TRUCKERS
THEY CROSSED THE CONTINENT OF HIS BED

Future imperfect will. She have? made gone. the dive for
his fresh superball eyes. He. will have forgot a. copied.
curiosity covered envelope. in black love scrawl
she never. Will.

have. pushed back curly curtains. to knock on his face.

Future indifferent: JUST SAY SO WHAT.
She will. or will not. mention
the three. Black kings. Sent. She thought,
by him. When she was abandoned. On the
island. Of his birth

VOW

Vow

What morning holds. . .
can never be hate
Maybe love, lust, or cloud

Tis possibility
Remnant of dream
Woven twixt shred of fact

Morning, though, can be mood

So I take the diurnal issue
tween arthritic palms
massage it with morning's prayer
neath shadow of night gone stale
whilst the fresh cracked day
looms
    its yellow life
    its golden threat
    its promise of lava
    sunbeams
    or chicks

So I take the new laid day
upon tender palms
Mold it
shape the day
From bed
like ancient hands
shift clay
and tender
What morning holds
I do

Signs of God and Art in Barcelona

all day over textured walks
the *bombonerías*, each a horizon

cielo in those storefronts, impressionist style
the pastels of *pasteles*
blend a creamy pink mauve mocha
crucifixion sunset
each blur of pastry emits
the urgent splendor of
a hallelujah choir

the omnipresent shank of pig
idol, fetish, counter display, sacrifice
scrape by scrape
with come and go customers

gypsies spit seeds, sell
dry white purple garlic slick yellow lemon
still lives on sun-cut corners

and pious coffee drinkers
flock to *café*
breathe clouds
I could go and be holy

another window
there's the hoof again

and proclaimed from high above
"*El Placer de Ser Mujer*"
   so let it be written
   so let it be done

Morning Prayer

Santosha[1] Sunrise
Bless me this breath
Shine light on my myriad shadows
Blanket me with love
Which I will cling to silkily
Beam me the courage to act and await
   the strength to give and forgive
   the grace to accept and receive
   the knowledge that BEING
      is always and ever
      within and around me
Remind me that JOY
   is the way
   to prance
   through the day
Melt my fears
   in your infinite warmth
And whisper to the sage inside
   to trust change
   for transformation crowns your golden embrace
I thank you
I thank you
   for all and every surprise
Santosha Sunrise

---

1. Santosha: the practice of contentedness in Vedanta philosophy

The Whispering Woods

What if a forest were an ocean of tethered souls
Not quite transcendent
Yet reaching for the heavens

waves of longing
course through the masses with every breeze

What if the woods were
An army of lost souls
Not (wicked) like those
doomed to smoldering worms
yet not conscious enough to soar
Like interstellar birds

What if those wisps of voice
One entertains as walking
The wood
Were the warnings to you and me
To cut all ties
To every item...
to all truck 'n mortar
Or remain rooted
beyond
our
sweet
demise

Palmistry

And if the stars
that decorate your
destiny
migrated
like hand-me-down toys
to frost generations
like disco-ball flecks
Would you cling to your path?
or starburst
till death?

The Cradle of My Mother's Hips

the cradle of my mother's hips
an audacity uncommon
in the hips of gringos
and white girls
a Jewish guitar twisting, Camden bred
like your cousin's piñata
that birthday, slugged at by every kid
in the family, still, a dangling dizzy rainbow
more delicious than the smashed buttercream
roses your tongue thorny for
the ice blue of my mother's
Siberian slant eyes blue hot
candles nobody can blow out
all else blanketed
in the conversation she lends
like library books if you're listening
if you read

All Hands

All hands on her
all hands in a well

Wash all hands
with her tears

Hold her, hands
lest she forget
her own walls

All hands over
the skin of her
milky wings

Touch the silken
hands of her
soul

Comfort Zone

There are:
Two kinds a people in the world:
   Those whose comfort zone is:
     In-the-know
   And those who feel secure in the:
     I-don't-know

Take *God* for instance

   There are the folks who are sure:
     She or He or It manages the multiverse

   They people the same category as
   Those who are just as certain:
     It's all a scam for the molten-minded
     There is, was, never has been nor will be
     Divinity

Then there are those of us
Who are sure only that:
   We are unsure:
     We could be:
       happy or unhappy accidental

Just as well:

     meticulously groomed integrated circuits compacted intricately crystalized inside a trajectory designed for ultimate evolution inscrutable learning opportunities by, for and with expanding consciousness that includes us, exudes us and for the here and now eludes us

Without Preaching

How do I say what I mean without preaching?
How do I express my exasperations without having a verbal fit?

How do I tell of my extreme, severe disappointment in the
human condition without supplicating?
Without begging you to feel me?
Be me?
See me?

How do I build a bridge with words if I'm not sure I want to
touch down on your land?
Or if I'm pretty sure you don't want to cross over to mine...

> For even the nanosecond a soul needs to cross over to the skin
> of another to seep in and sip the air and soak in the personal
> history and listen with the soft openness of ears hearing the
> distant calls of lost creatures in a dark forest

I need to make a pact that I will go to your forest
That I will listen to the darkness
to the invisible sounds

I think this might be the only way
I can tell you things

At Night

I pull on the sparkling
udders of the sky

bittersweet night juice

runs past my elbows
it's indigo
splashes in my eye

tastes like India ink

of a hundred thousand poets times love
whose pens through the ages
milked the night sky
for truth

ABOUT THE AUTHOR

Tamra Plotnick has work in a variety of journals and anthologies, including *Serving House Journal*; *The Waiting Room Reader, Vol II: Words to Keep You Company*, edited by Rachel Hadas; *Tribes #8, Stickman Review, LiveMag, BigCityLit; Atlantic Review; Lurch; Burrow; The Midwest Review; Hunger Enough*, and *Global City Review: International Edition*. Her memoir excerpt "Barbie and Gandhi Sitting in a Tree" appeared in *The Coachella Review*. She has read and performed her work in multi-media shows at various venues, including La Mama Theater, Zinc Bar, KGB, and Cornelia Street Café. With a long and varied background as a dancer, Tamra has performed at Dixon Place, Café Teatro Julia de Burgos, The Caribbean Cultural Center, and PS 122. She has developed and led workshops melding creative writing with movement and continues to dance samba, Afro-Caribbean, improvisation, and raqs sharqi. Tamra earned a master's degree in Creative Writing from City College of New York, where she won a New York Times Fellowship and an undergraduate degree from Sarah Lawrence College. Additionally, she holds a master's degree in education and is a certified yoga instructor. She teaches English Language Arts in an alternative public high school in Manhattan and lives with her family in Brooklyn.

www.tamraplotnick.net

www.ingramcontent.com/pod-product-compliance
Lightning Source LLC
Chambersburg PA
CBHW030308100526
44590CB00012B/568